70 Repas Paléo Hautement Protéinés:

Recettes de Repas Hautement Protéinés sans Suppléments ou Pilules pour Augmenter la Masse Musculaire

Par

Joseph Correa
Nutritionniste Certifié des Sportifs

DROITS D'AUTEUR

© 2015 Correa Media Group

Tous droits réservés

La reproduction ou la traduction de toute partie de ce travail au-delà de ce qui est permis par l'article 107 ou 108 de la Loi de 1976 sur les droits d'auteur aux États-Unis 1976, sans l'autorisation préalable du propriétaire des droits d'auteur, est illégale.

Cette publication est conçue pour fournir des informations exactes et faisant autorité en ce qui concerne le sujet traité. Cette publication est vendue avec la condition implicite que ni l'auteur ni l'éditeur n'ont la capacité de prodiguer des conseils médicaux. Si des conseils ou une assistance médicale se déclarent nécessaires, vous êtes priés de consulter un médecin. Ce livre est considéré comme un guide et ne doit être utilisé en aucune façon nuisible à votre santé. Consultez un médecin avant de commencer ce plan nutritionnel pour vous assurer qu'il vous sera bénéfique.

REMERCIEMENTS

La réalisation et le succès de ce livre n'auraient pu être possibles sans le soutien et l'aide précieuse de ma famille.

70 Repas Paléo Hautement Protéinés :

Recettes de Repas Hautement Protéinés sans Suppléments ou Pilules pour Augmenter la Masse Musculaire

Par

Joseph Correa
Nutritionniste Certifié des Sportifs

SOMMAIRE

Droits d'Auteur

Remerciements

À Propos de l'Auteur

Introduction

70 Repas Paléo Hautement Protéinés :
Recettes de Repas Hautement Protéinés sans Suppléments ou Pilules pour Augmenter la Masse Musculaire

Autres Grands Titres de cet Auteur

À PROPOS DE L'AUTEUR

En tant que nutritionniste certifié des sportifs et athlète professionnel, je crois fermement qu'une bonne nutrition vous aidera à atteindre vos objectifs plus rapidement et plus efficacement. Mes connaissances et mon expérience m'ont permis de vivre en meilleure santé tout au long des années et je l'ai partagé avec ma famille et mes amis. Plus vous en savez à propos de boire et vous nourrir plus sainement, et le plus tôt vous aurez envie de changer votre vie et vos habitudes alimentaires.

Réussir à contrôler votre poids est très important, car cela vous permettra d'améliorer tous les aspects de votre vie.

La nutrition est un élément clé dans le processus de se mettre en meilleure forme et c'est là tout le sujet de ce livre.

INTRODUCTION

70 Repas Paléo Hautement Protéinés :
Recettes de Repas Hautement Protéinés sans Suppléments ou Pilules pour Augmenter la Masse Musculaire

Ce livre va vous aider à augmenter l'apport de protéines que vous consommez par jour pour vous aider à augmenter votre masse musculaire. Ces repas vous aideront à augmenter vos muscles d'une manière organisée en ajoutant une grande quantité de protéines saines à votre régime. Être trop occupé pour manger correctement peut devenir parfois un problème, c'est pourquoi ce livre va vous faire gagner du temps et vous aidera à nourrir votre corps pour atteindre les buts que vous recherchez. Assurez-vous que vous savez ce que vous mangez en préparant les repas vous-mêmes ou en les faisant préparer par quelqu'un pour vous.

Ce livre vous aidera à :

-Augmenter vos muscles rapidement et naturellement.

-Améliorer la récupération musculaire.

-Avoir plus d'énergie.

-Accélérer naturellement votre métabolisme pour construire plus de muscles.

-Améliorer votre système digestif.

Joseph Correa est un nutritionniste certifié des sportifs et un athlète professionnel.

Calendrier pour 70 Repas Paléo Hautement Protéinés

JOUR	PETIT-DEJEUNER	SNACK	DEJEUNER	SNACK	DINER
1.	2 oeufs durs avec du basilic haché	1 pamplemousse	1 beef sirloin with slices of eggplant	1 cup of tomato and walnuts salad	1 cup of cooked chard with olive oil
2.	½ tasse de champignons cuits au romarin	1 poire	1 cup of octopus salad with tomatoes and capers	1 cup of roasted almonds	1 grilled zucchini with garlic and parsley
3.	1 verre de shake de fruits et de légumes mélangés	1 verre de jus d'abricot frais	2 cups of fish stew	1 peach	1 cup of fresh fruits of your choice
4.	½ tasse d'omelette d'ananas aux amandes	1 orange	1 beef chop with pineapple and tumeric	1 cup of chopped cucumber with fennel	2 apples
5.	1 tasse de salade de fruits	1 tasse d' de salade de thon avec de la laitue au curry	1 turkey drumstick with nutmeg and carob	3 grilled eggplant slices with chopped fennel	1 cup of octopus salad with tomatoes and capers
6.	1 tasse d'omelette d'épinards	1 verre de jus d'ananas frais, sans sucre	1 medium piece of eggplant casserole	1 cup of cooked leek with lemon sauce	2 boiled eggs with grated ginger
7.	1 tasse de salade de tomates et de noix	1 tasse de champignons cuits avec des légumes et sauce au gingembre	3 chicken wings with tumeric sauce	1 cup of tomato and tuna salad	1 veal steak with red pepper sauce
8.	½ tasse d' omelette aux champignons	1 verre de jus de canneberges fraîches	2 turkey fillet with walnuts and maple syrup	2 boiled eggs	1 cup of roasted cherry tomatoes, eggplant and basil salad
9.	½ cup of nutmeg omelet	1 tasse de crevettes à la sauce tomate	1 cup of lettuce salad	5 dried plums	1 cup of coriander salad
10.	2 fried eggs with chopped mint	1 tasse de salade de thon avec de la laitue au curry	1 veal chop with chopped cloves	1 cup of tomato soup	2 boiled eggs with chopped coriander

70 Repas Paléo Hautement Protéinés

11.	3 pineapple slices with grated almonds	1 courgettes grillée au basilic et a la menthe hachée	1 cup of chopped veal soup with vegetables	2 cooked carrots	1 cup of grapes
12.	1 cup of cooked broccoli	2 tasses de salade de fruits	1 lamb cutlet with hazelnut sauce	1 grilled red pepper	1 cooked potato in parsley sauce
13.	1 cup of eggplant pate	1 tasse de laitue et salade de thon	½ cup of stewed beef and cabbage	1 cup of broccoli soup	1 cup of roasted almonds
14.	1 glass of fresh orange juice	½ tasse de noix de Grenoble	1 grilled trout fillets with parsley	1 cup of fresh cranberries and grated walnuts	1 cup of cauliflower soup
15.	½ cup of tomato omelet	1 tasse de baies	1 grilled salmon fillet	2 carrots	1 cup of roasted almonds
16.	1 glass of fresh orange and lime juice	1 tasse de salade de légumes mélangés	1 cup of grilled calamari in curry sauce	3 fresh figs	2 grilled sardines
17.	1 glass of banana shake	2 poivrons verts grillés	1 cup of seafood salad	2 baked apples	1 grilled zucchini with garlic
18.	2 boiled eggs	1 poire et amandes grillées	1 grilled steak with pineapple slices	1 cup of cooked cauliflower in mint sauce	1 grated apple with walnuts and cinnamon
19.	1 cup of mushroom soup	1 trout fillet with almond and tumeric sauce	1 cup of trout soup	1 cup of cucumber salad	½ cup of grilled mushrooms with garlic sauce
20.	1 glass of fresh lime juice	2 cups of cooked, canned broccoli	1 beef chop with pineapple and tumeric	1 glass of fresh tomato juice	2 grilled sardines
21.	3 apple and carrot balls with cinnamon	1 grilled eggplant with parsley	1 cup of steak salad with mushrooms	1 cooked carrot	1 sour asparagus
22.	1 glass of fruit shake	3 grilled eggplant slices	1 veal cutlet with almonds	1 cup of berries and Brazil nuts	2 grilled red peppers
23.	½ cup of spinach omelet	1 cup tomato and garlic soup	2 squids stuffed with walnuts	1 glass of fresh lemonade	½ cup of Brazil nuts

70 Repas Paléo Hautement Protéinés

24.	1 banana	1 cup of lettuce and tuna salad	1 lamb cutlet with basil	1 cucumber	1 cup of grilled mushrooms in tomato sauce
25.	2 fried eggs	½ cup of Brazil and Macadamia nuts	1 cup of shrimp skewers	1 cup of cooked broccoli	1 glass of fresh vegetable juice of your choice
26.	3 pineapple slices with grated almonds	1 cup of broccoli soup	2 turkey fillet with walnuts and maple syrup salmon in almond sauce	1 cup of lettuce and cherry tomato salad	1 apple
27.	1 glass of fresh carrot juice	1 cup of cucumber salad	1 beef chop with pineapple and tumeric	1 cup of chopped cucumber with fennel	1 cup of cooked leek with lemon sauce
28.	1 cup of tomato and walnuts salad	1 glass of fresh apricot juice	2 cups of fish stew	3 dried plums	1 cup of trout soup
29.	3 apple and carrot balls with cinnamon	1 grilled zucchini with chopped basil and mint	1 beef chop with pineapple and tumeric	1 cup of roasted almonds	1 cup of octopus salad with tomatoes and capers
30.	1 cup of eggplant pate	1 cup of cooked mushrooms with vegetables and ginger sauce	1 medium piece of eggplant casserole	1 glass of lemonade without sugar	1 cup of roasted cherry tomatoes, eggplant and basil salad

70 HIGH PROTEIN PALEO MEALS

1. Boiled eggs with chopped basil

Ingredients:

2 eggs

1 tsp of chopped basil

pepper

Preparation:

Boil eggs for 10 minutes. Peel and chop into small pieces. Sprinkle with chopped basil.

Nutritional values per 100 g:

Carbohydrates 1.1g

Sugar 0g

Protein 13g

Total fat (good monounsaturated fat) 11g

Sodium 124mg

Potassium 126mg

Calcium 50mg

Iron 1.2mg

Vitamins (vitamin A; B-6; B-12; C)

Calories 155

2. Beef sirloin with slices of eggplant

Ingredients:

1 thin beef sirloin

1 medium eggplant

1 tsp of olive oil

chopped basil

pepper

Preparation:

Wash and pepper the meat. Grill it on a barbecue pan for about 10 minutes on each side. Remove from pan. Peel eggplant and cut two thick slices. Fry for few minutes in the same barbecue pan. Remove from heat and serve with beef. Sprinkle with chopped basil.

Nutritional values:

Carbohydrates 6g

Sugar 1.2g

Protein 35.2 g

Total fat 4.9g

Sodium 57 mg

Potassium 397mg

Calcium 18.5mg

Iron 1.9mg

Vitamins (vitamin A; B-6; B-12; C; D; D2; D3; K;Thiamin; K)

Calories 212

3. Tomato and walnuts salad

Ingredients:

1 big tomato

½ cup of chopped walnuts

1 tsp of lemon juice

Preparation:

Wash and cut tomato into small pieces. Add chopped walnuts and mix well. Pour lemon juice over it.

Nutritional values for 1 cup:

Carbohydrates 8.2g

Sugar 3.8g

Protein 10g

Total fat 4.5g

Sodium 17 mg

Potassium 112mg

Calcium 16.5mg

Iron 1.3mg

Vitamins (vitamin A; B-6; B-12; C; D; D2; D3; K; Riboflavin; Niacin; Thiamin; K)

Calories 218

4. Cooked chard with olive oil

Ingredients:

1 bunch of chard

1 tsp of olive oil

1 tsp of tumeric

Preparation:

Wash and chop chard. Fry it in olive oil for 20 minutes on a low temperature, or until tender. Add tumeric before serving.

Nutritional values for one cup:

Carbohydrates 6.9g

Sugar 2.1g

Protein 8.4 g

Total fat 1.9g

Sodium 34.2 mg

Potassium 23.2mg

Calcium 12.4mg

Iron 0.59mg

Vitamins (vitamin A; B-6; B-12; C; D; D2; D3; K; Riboflavin; Niacin; Thiamin; K)

Calories 113

5. Baked mushrooms with rosemary

Ingredients:

1 cup of mushrooms

1 tsp of olive oil

1 tsp of chopped rosemary

Preparation:

Bake mushrooms in a barbecue pan for 5-7 minutes. Remove from pan and sprinkle with olive oil and chopped rosemary.

Nutritional values for one cup:

Carbohydrates 6.2g

Sugar 1.1g

Protein 8.4 g

Total fat (good monounsaturated fat) 1.3g

Sodium 48.2 mg

Potassium 23.2mg

Calcium 12.4mg

Iron 0.59mg

Vitamins (vitamin A; B-6; B-12; C; D; D2; D3; K; Riboflavin; Niacin; Thiamin; K)

Calories 117

6. Octopus salad with tomatoes and capers

Ingredients:

1 cup of frozen cut octopus

¼ cup of capers

½ cup of olives

5 cherry tomatoes

1 tsp of chopped parsley

1 tsp of chopped celery

1 small onion

2 cloves of garlic

1 tsp of chopped rosemary

1 tbsp of olive oil

1 tsp of lemon juice

Preparation:

Cook the octopus in salted water until tender. It usually takes about 20-30 minutes. Remove from pot, wash and drain. Wash and cut vegetables and mix with octopus. Mix the spices and add to salad. Sprinkle with olive oil and lemon juice. Cool well before serving.

Nutritional values for one cup:

Carbohydrates 12.9g

Sugar 5.1g

Protein 16.4 g

Total fat (good monounsaturated fat) 9.9g

Sodium 114.2 mg

Potassium 83.2mg

Calcium 42.4mg

Iron 0.59mg

Vitamins (vitamin A; B-6; B-12; C; D; D2; D3; K; Riboflavin; Niacin; Thiamin; K)

Calories 81

7. Grilled zucchini with garlic and parsley

Ingredients:

1 medium zucchini

1 tbsp of chopped parsley

2 cloves of garlic

Preparation:

Peel the zucchini and cut into 4 slices. Fry in a barbecue pan for 3-4 minutes. Add chopped garlic and bake for another 5 minutes. Sprinkle with parsley before serving.

Nutritional values:

Carbohydrates 3.71g

Sugar 3g

Protein 2 g

Total fat 0g

Sodium 2.9 mg

Potassium 360mg

Calcium 0.2mg

Iron 0.3mg

Vitamins (vitamin A; B-6; B-12; C; D:K)

Calories 20

8. Mixed fruits and vegetables shake

Ingredients:

1 cup of mixed blueberries, raspberries, blackberries and strawberries

½ cup of chopped baby spinach

2 cups of water

Preparation:

Mix ingredients in a blender for few minutes.

Nutritional values for 1 cup:

Carbohydrates 9.2g

Sugar 6.15g

Protein 8.75g

Total fat 0.87g

Sodium 54.8mg

Potassium 107.8mg

Calcium 82mg

Iron 2.03mg

Vitamins (Vitamin C total ascorbic acid; B-6; B-12; Folate-DFE; A-RAE; A-IU; E-alpha-tocopherol; D; D-D2+D3; K-phylloquinone; Thianin; Riboflavin; Niacin)

Calories 42.6

9. Fish stew

Ingredients:

1 carp fillet

1 carrot

2 chili peppers

1 medium tomato

pepper

celery roots and leaf

Preparation:

It is the best to buy cooked carrots, or cook them before preparing the fish stew. Wash and cut vegetables, mix with celery and fish and put in a pot. Pour little water, just to cover it. Cook on a low temperature for 20-30 minutes.

Nutritional values:

Carbohydrates 8.2g

Sugar 3.9g

Protein 15.2 g

Total fat (good monounsaturated fat) 6.6g

Sodium 113.8 mg

Potassium 71mg

Calcium 29.1mg

Iron 0.32mg

Vitamins (vitamin A; B-6; B-12; C; D; D2; D3; K; Riboflavin; Niacin; Thiamin; K)

Calories 172

10. Pineapple omelet with almonds

Ingredients:

3 slices of pineapple

2 eggs

½ cup of almonds

1 tbsp of flaxseed oil for frying

Preparation:

Beat the eggs and add almonds. Fry pineapple slices for few minutes on both sides, without oil. When done, remove from pan, add oil, heat it and add eggs mixture. Serve with baked pineapple slices.

Nutritional values per 100g:

Carbohydrates 8.9g

Sugar 4.6g

Protein 19.2 g

Total fat 13.6g

Sodium 134.8 mg

Potassium 131mg

Calcium 67.1mg

Iron 1.52mg

Vitamins (vitamin A; B-12; C; K; Riboflavin; Niacin; K)

Calories 187

11. Beef chop with pineapple and tumeric

Ingredients:

1 medium beef chop

1 tbsp of olive oil

1 tsp of tumeric

Pepper

2 pineapple slices

Preparation:

Wash and dry the meat. Fry it without oil, in it's own sauce, for 15-20 minutes on low temperature. Remove from heat. Make a sauce with olive oil, tumeric and pepper and spread it over fried beef. Fry it once more for 3-4 minutes, add pineapple slices and serve warm.

Nutritional values per 100g:

Carbohydrates 15.7g

Sugar 9.9g

Protein 34g

Total fat (good monounsaturated fat) 17.6g

Sodium 99.3 mg

Potassium 328mg

Calcium 49.1mg

Iron 0.52mg

Vitamins (vitamin A; B-6; B-12; C; D; D2; D3; K; Riboflavin; Niacin; Thiamin; K)

Calories 311

12. Fruit salad

Ingredients:

1 cup of berries

½ cup of pineapple cubes

½ cup of chopped apple

1 tsp of cinnamon

1 tsp of agave syrup

Preparation:

Mix fruits, add agave syrup and sprinkle with cinnamon.

Nutritional values for one cup:

Carbohydrates 19.2g

Sugar 12g

Protein 15.2 g

Total fat (good monounsaturated fat) 4.6g

Sodium 123.8 mg

Potassium 95mg

Calcium 44.1mg

Iron 0.52mg

Vitamins (vitamin A; B-6; B-12; C; D; D2; D3; K; Riboflavin; Niacin; Thiamin; K)

Calories 77

13. Tuna salad with lettuce and curry

Ingredients:

1 small can of tuna without oil

1 bunch of lettuce

2 chili peppers

1 tsp of curry

1 tsp of lemon sauce

Preparation:

Wash and cut lettuce. Mix it with tuna, add chopped chili peppers and lemon sauce. Sprinkle with curry.

Nutritional values for 1 cup:

Carbohydrates 23.4g

Sugar 13g

Protein 33.2g

Total fat (good monounsaturated fat) 12.4g

Sodium 123mg

Potassium 72.3mg

Calcium 42.1mg

Iron 0.27mg

Vitamins (vitamin A; B-6; B-12; C; D; D2; D3; K; Riboflavin; Niacin; Thiamin; K)

Calories 68

14. Turkey drumstick with nutmeg and carob

Ingredients:

1 turkey drumstick

½ cup of water

½ cup of nutmeg

½ cup of carob

Preparation:

Wash and clean the meat. Fry it for about 15 minutes in it's own sauce (add some water while frying the turkey). Finely chop nutmeg and carob and add to saucepan. Mix well with turkey sauce. Remove from the pan and sprinkle with some more carob.

Nutritional values for one cup:

Carbohydrates 3.2g

Sugar 0.9g

Protein 31g

Total fat (good monounsaturated fat) 10.4g

Sodium 998mg

Potassium 78.2mg

Calcium 48mg

Iron 0.37mg

Vitamins (vitamin A; B-6; B-12; C; D; D2; D3; K; Riboflavin; Niacin; Thiamin; K)

Calories 210

15. Grilled eggplant slices with chopped fennel

Ingredients:

1 large eggplant

½ cup of chopped fennel

1 tbsp of olive oil

1 tsp of chopped parsley

Preparation:

Peel the eggplant and cut into 3 slices. Bake it in a barbecue pan without oil. When done, spread olive oil over it, sprinkle with fennel and parsley.

(These eggplant slices are great cold, so you can leave them overnight in a refrigerator)

Nutritional values per slice:

Carbohydrates 8.9g

Sugar 3g

Protein 7g

Total fat (good monounsaturated fat) 2.4g

Sodium 54mg

Potassium 32.5mg

Calcium 12.4mg

Iron 0.37mg

Vitamins (vitamin A; B-6; B-12; C; D; D2; D3; K; Riboflavin; Niacin; Thiamin; K)

Calories 54

16. Spinach omelet

Ingredients:

1 cup of chopped spinach

2 eggs

1 tbsp of olive oil for frying

Preparation:

Cook spinach in salted water until tender. Remove from pan and drain. Fry in olive oil for 5-6 minutes and add eggs. Mix well and serve warm.

Nutritional values per 100g:

Carbohydrates 1.9g

Sugar 0.6g

Protein 19.2 g

Total fat 13.6g

Sodium 144mg

Potassium 133mg

Calcium 71mg

Iron 1.8mg

Vitamins (vitamin A; B-12; C; K; Riboflavin; Niacin; K)

Calories 177

17. Eggplant casserole

Ingredients:

2 large eggplants

1 cup of minced meat

1 medium onion

1 tsp of olive oil

pepper

2 medium tomatoes

1 tsp of chopped parsley

Preparation:

Peel the eggplants and cut lengthwise into thin sheets. Put them in a bowl, and leave them to sit for at least an hour. Roll them in beaten eggs. Fry in hot oil. Cut the onion, fry, add sliced peppers, tomato, which is cut into cubes, and finely chopped parsley. Fry for few minutes and then add the meat. When meat is tender, remove from heat, cool, add 1 egg and season with pepper. Put fried eggplant and meat with vegetables in an ovenproof dish and make layers until you have used all the material. Bake for 30 minutes at 300 degrees.

Nutritional values per 100g:

Carbohydrates 7.9g

Sugar 3.4g

Protein 10.2 g

Total fat 13.6g

Sodium 164mg

Potassium 302mg

Calcium 21.1mg

Iron 1.32mg

Vitamins (vitamin A; B-12; C; K; Riboflavin; Niacin; K)

Calories 109

18. Leek with chicken cubes

Ingredients:

2 cups of trimmed leeks

1 cup of chicken fillets, cut into cubes

olive oil

thyme leaves for decoration

salt to taste

Preparation:

Cut the leeks into small pieces and wash it under cold water, day before serving. Leave it overnight in a plastic bag.

Heat the oil in a large pan. Add chicken cubes and fry for about 15 minutes on a medium temperature. Add leaks, mix well and fry for another 10 minutes on a low temperature. Remove from the saucepan and allow it to cool. Decorate with thyme leaves.

Nutritional values for 1 cup:

Carbohydrates 7g

Sugar 1.6g

Protein 18.1 g

Total fat 13.6g

Sodium 124.1 mg

Potassium 120mg

Calcium 69.3mg

Iron 1.42mg

Vitamins (vitamin A; B-6; B-12; C; D; D2; D3; K; Riboflavin; Niacin; Thiamin; K)

Calories 187

19. Cooked mushrooms with vegetables

Ingredients:

2 cups of button mushrooms

1 cup of dried turkey cubes

2 large carrots

½ cup of chopped cabbage

1 tsp of ginger

1 tbsp of olive oil

1 tsp of chopped parsley

Preparation:

Cook vegetables in water until tender. Remove from pan and drain. Allow it to cool for a while. Mix olive oil, ginger and parsley, add little water and cook it for few minutes, on a medium heat. Pour over vegetables, add dried turkey and mix well. Allow it to cool in the refrigerator for about 30 minutes before serving.

Nutritional values for 1 cup:

Carbohydrates 18.6g

Sugar 11.3g

Protein 21.9g

Total fat 14.2g

Sodium 153.3 mg

Potassium 89.8mg

Calcium 49.9mg

Iron 0.42mg

Vitamins (vitamin A; B-6; B-12; C; D; D2; D3; K; Riboflavin; Niacin; Thiamin; K)

Calories 79

20. Chicken wings with tumeric sauce

Ingredients:

2 chicken wings

1 tsp of tumeric

1 tbsp of olive oil

½ tsp of dried rosemary

¼ tsp of red pepper

Preparation:

Fry chicken wings in a barbecue pan for 10-15 minutes. 3-4 minutes before chicken is done, add olive oil, tumeric, rosemary, pepper and a little water. Mix well the sauce and soak the chicken in it.

Nutritional values per 100g:

Carbohydrates 18.6g

Sugar 0.9g

Protein 28g

Total fat 22.7g

Sodium 431.3 mg

Potassium 189mg

Calcium 2.9mg

Iron 2.42mg

Vitamins (vitamin A; B-6; B-12; C; D; D2; D3; K; Riboflavin; Niacin; Thiamin; K)

Calories 318

21. Tomato and tuna salad

Ingredients:

2 large tomatoes

2 medium onions

3 cans of tuna

1 tbsp of olive oil

1 tsp of lemon juice

basil

salt to taste

Preparation:

Wash and peel the vegetables. Cut it into small cubes. Add olive oil, lemon juice and basil. Mix well.

Nutritional values for one cup:

Carbohydrates 17.9g

Sugar 9.1g

Protein 28.3 g

Total fat (good monounsaturated fat) 15.8g

Sodium 127mg

Potassium 89.6mg

Calcium 42.1mg

Iron 0.38mg

Vitamins (vitamin A; B-6; B-12; C; D; D2; D3; K; Riboflavin; Niacin; Thiamin; K)

Calories 99

22. Veal steak with red pepper sauce

Ingredients:

1 medium veal steak

1 large red paprika

1 tsp of red pepper

1 tbsp of olive oil

chopped rosemary

Preparation:

Wash and cut paprika into small pieces. Put in a large pan, add olive oil and rosemary. Stew for 15 minutes on low heat. Add red pepper and cook for another few minutes. Wash and dry the steak. Fry it in a barbecue pan until tender. Add sauce and remove from pan.

Nutritional values per 100g:

Carbohydrates 4.5g

Sugar 2.1g

Protein 26 g

Total fat 9.8g

Sodium 87 mg

Potassium 339mg

Calcium 2.1mg

Iron 0.16mg

Vitamins (vitamin A; B-6; B-12; C; D; D2; D3; K)

Calories 203

23. Mushroom omelet

Ingredients:

1 cup of mushrooms,

2 eggs

1 tbsp of olive oil

Preparation:

Fry the mushrooms in olive oil on a low temperature. Let the mushroom sauce evaporate. Add eggs and mix well.

Nutritional values per 100 g:

Carbohydrates 4.1g

Sugar 0g

Protein 18g

Total fat (good monounsaturated fat) 11g

Sodium 126mg

Potassium 124mg

Calcium 14.9mg

Iron 1.8mg

Vitamins (vitamin A; B-6; B-12; C)

Calories 174

24. Turkey fillet with walnuts and maple syrup

Ingredients:

3 turkey fillets

½ cup of walnuts

1 tsp of maple syrup

¼ cup of water

1 tbsp of olive oil

salt to taste

Preparation:

Fry the fillets in a barbecue pan on a low temperature for about 15 minutes, or until tender. Remove from the heath and add water, maple syrup and walnuts. Mix well and fry for another 5-6 minutes until the water evaporates. Allow it to cool for a while.

Nutritional values per 100 g:

Carbohydrates 10.1g

Sugar 7.3g

Protein 24.2g

Total fat 8.7g

Sodium 1025mg

Potassium 126mg

Calcium 50mg

Iron 1.2mg

Vitamins (vitamin A; B-6; C)

Calories 148

25. Roasted cherry tomatoes, eggplant and basil salad

Ingredients:

1 small eggplant

5 egg whites

1 cup of cherry tomatoes

1 tsp of fresh chopped basil

1 tbsp of olive oil

white pepper to taste

1 tsp of lemon juice

Preparation:

Cut eggplant into thick pieces, dice shape. Salt the eggplant cubes, add oil, egg whites and place on a baking sheet. If necessary, add some more olive oil (this is optional). Bake for about 10 minutes in preheated oven at 350 degrees. Clean the cherry tomatoes and fry for about 15 minutes on a low temperature, using a small saucepan. You want to get lightly caramelized tomato sauce.
Remove from the heath and allow it to cool for a while. Gently stir in the lemon sauce, olive oil and fresh basil.

Pour over the eggplant and serve cold. A great side dish with barbecue or grilled fish. You can keep it in the fridge up to one week.

Nutritional values per slice:

Carbohydrates 10.4g

Sugar 3g

Protein 19g

Total fat (good monounsaturated fat) 4.9g

Sodium 52mg

Potassium 38.3mg

Calcium 12.9mg

Iron 0.32mg

Vitamins (vitamin A; B-6; B-12; C; D; D2; D3; K; Riboflavin; Niacin; Thiamin; K)

Calories 87

26. Nutmeg omelet

Ingredients:

3 eggs

2 tbsp of olive oil

1 tsp of nutmeg

1/5 tsp of pepper

Preparation:

Beat the eggs and add nutmeg and pepper. Mix well and fry in olive oil for few minutes. Serve warm. You can add some salt if you like.

Nutritional values per 100g:

Carbohydrates 0.9g

Sugar 0.45g

Protein 12g

Total fat 12.4g

Sodium 156mg

Potassium 117.5mg

Calcium 4.4mg

Iron 7.37mg

Vitamins (vitamin A; B-6; D; D2; D3)

Calories 156

27. Shrimps in tomato sauce

Ingredients:

2 cups of frozen shrimps

1 large tomato

1 tsp of dried basil

2 cloves of garlic

3 tbsp of olive oil

salt to taste

Preparation:

Grill frozen shrimps in a barbecue pan without oil. Wash and cut tomato into small pieces, add chopped basil, chopped garlic and olive oil. Cook it for 5-6 minutes (add some water if necessary). Pour the sauce over the grilled shrimps. Serve with lettuce.

Nutritional values per 100g:

Carbohydrates 7.9g

Sugar 4.2g

Protein 28g

Total fat (good monounsaturated fat) 1.32g

Sodium 131mg

Potassium 269.5mg

Calcium 8.7mg

Iron 4.37mg

Vitamins (vitamin A; B-6; B-12; C; D; D2; D3; K; Riboflavin; Niacin; Thiamin; K)

Calories 164

28. Lettuce salad

Ingredients:

1 bunch of lettuce

1 tbsp of olive oil

1 tsp of lemon juice

Preparation:

Wash and cut the lettuce, add olive oil and lemon juice. It is the best to prepare this salad before serving a meal. Don't let it stand long.

Nutritional values per 1 cup:

Carbohydrates 1.2g

Sugar 0.3g

Protein 1.7g

Total fat (good monounsaturated fat) 1.4g

Sodium 19mg

Potassium 132mg

Calcium 1.4mg

Iron 2.3mg

Vitamins (vitamin A; B-6; B-12; C;K)

Calories 25

29. Coriander salad

Ingredients:

1 cup of chopped coriander

1 boiled egg

2 cups of cherry tomatoes

1 tsp of tumeric

2 tbsp of olive oil

1 tsp of lemon sauce

salt to taste

Preparation:

Wash and cut cherry tomatoes and mix with coriander. Add tumeric, olive oil and lemon sauce.

Nutritional values for one cup:

Carbohydrates 14.2g

Sugar 8.9g

Protein 10g

Total fat (good monounsaturated fat) 9.6g

Sodium 122.2 mg

Potassium 81mg

Calcium 45.5mg

Iron 0.37mg

Vitamins (vitamin A; B-6; B-12; C; D; D2; D3; K; Riboflavin; Niacin; Thiamin; K)

Calories 55

30. Fried eggs with chopped mint

Ingredients:

3 eggs

1 tbsp of olive oil

1 tbsp of chopped mint

1 cup of cherry tomatoes

1 small onion

pepper to taste

salt to taste

Preparation:

Cut the vegetables into small pieces and fry in large saucepan on a low temperature for about 15 minutes. Wait for the water to evaporate. Beat the eggs and add chopped mint. Mix with vegetables, add olive oil and fry for few minutes. Before serving add some salt and pepper to taste.

Nutritional values per 100 g:

Carbohydrates 8.1g

Sugar 4g

Protein 28g

Total fat (good monounsaturated fat) 11.9g

Sodium 176mg

Potassium 174mg

Calcium 17.9mg

Iron 1.5mg

Vitamins (vitamin A; B-6; B-12; C; D; D2; D3; K; Riboflavin; Niacin; Thiamin; K)

Calories 194

31. Veal chop with chopped cloves

Ingredients:

2 large veal chops

1 cup of chopped cloves

4 tbsp of olive oil

1 tbsp of dried parsley

1 tsp of rosemary

1 tsp of red pepper

1 tbsp of lemon juice

Preparation:

Mix well the cloves, olive oil, parsley and rosemary to get a nice sauce. Wash the steak and put it in a small baking tray. Add sauce and bake for 15-20 minutes at 300 degrees. Remove from the oven, sprinkle with pepper and lemon juice. Decorate with few parsley leaves. Allow it to cool for about 10 minutes.

Nutritional values per 100g:

Carbohydrates 8.2g

Sugar 4.9g

Protein 22g

Total fat 9.6g

Sodium 97.2 mg

Potassium 381mg

Calcium 4.5mg

Iron 5.3mg

Vitamins (vitamin A; B-6; B-12; C; D; D2; D3; K; Riboflavin; Niacin; Thiamin; K)

Calories 216

32. Tomato soup

Ingredients:

1 cup of tomato sauce

2 egg whites

2 cups of water

2 cloves of garlic

2 tbsp of olive oil

1tsp of dried marjoram

chopped parsley

Preparation:

Fry finely chopped garlic in oil. Stir in tomato sauce mixed with water. Add parsley and let it boil. Serve with marjoram.

Nutritional values per 150ml:

Carbohydrates 6.8g

Sugar 3.9g

Protein 7g

Total fat (good monounsaturated fat) 0.6g

Sodium 190.2 mg

Potassium 112mg

Calcium 0.5mg

Iron 2.3mg

Vitamins (vitamin A; C)

Calories 30

33. Grilled zucchini with chopped basil and mint

Ingredients:

1 large zucchini

¼ cup of chopped basil

¼ cup of chopped mint

1 tbsp of olive oil

¼ glass of water,

pepper to taste

Preparation:

Cook spices in water and add pepper for 2-3 minutes. Peel and cut zucchini into three slices. Grill it in a barbecue pan with olive oil. Add mint and basil. Fry until all the water evaporates. You can add some lemon juice before serving, but this is optional.

Nutritional values for 1 slice:

Carbohydrates 3.8g

Sugar 2g

Protein 2.9 g

Total fat 0.9g

Sodium 2.76 mg

Potassium 343mg

Calcium 0.27mg

Iron 0.3mg

Vitamins (vitamin A; B-6; B-12; C; D:K)

Calories 23

34. Chopped veal soup with vegetables

Ingredients:

1 thick veal steak

2 large carrots

½ cup of chopped parsley

1 large tomato

¼ tsp of pepper

1 small onion

Preparation:

Wash the meat and put it in a pot. Pour water and cook until meat is tender. Meanwhile, clean and cut the vegetables into small cubes. When the meat is cooked, remove it from the pan and cut it into small cubes. Mix with vegetables, return to the water and cook until carrots are tender. Add seasoning and serve.

Nutritional values per 1 cup:

Carbohydrates 3g

Sugar 2.1g

Protein 22 g

Total fat 5.7g

Sodium 71 mg

Potassium 148mg

Calcium 2.2mg

Iron 4.3mg

Vitamins (vitamin A; B-6; B-12; C; D; D2; D3; K; Riboflavin; Niacin; Thiamin; K)

Calories 112

35. Lamb cutlet with hazelnut sauce

Ingredients:

1 medium lamb cutlet

½ cup of hazelnuts

1 tsp of curry

1 tbsp of olive oil

pepper to taste

Preparation:

Wash the cutlet and cook in water 15-20 minutes. Remove from pot and drain, but keep the water. Make a sauce with olive oil, curry, hazelnuts and pepper. Spread the sauce over cutlet, add some meat water and bake at 300 degrees for 15-20 minutes.

Nutritional values per 100g:

Carbohydrates 4.7g

Sugar 4.1g

Protein 29 g

Total fat 11.8g

Sodium 137 mg

Potassium 239mg

Calcium 2.9mg

Iron 2.16mg

Vitamins (vitamin A; B-6; B-12; C; D; D2; D3; K; Riboflavin; Niacin; Thiamin; K)

Calories 213

36. Grilled red pepper

Ingredients:

1 large red pepper

1 tbsp of olive oil

2 cloves of garlic

chopped parsley

Preparation:

Mix olive oil with garlic and parsley. Spread the sauce over paprika and bake in barbecue pan on low temperature for about 10-15 minutes.

Nutritional values per 100g:

Carbohydrates 6.2g

Sugar 4.4g

Protein 2g

Total fat 0.8g

Sodium 7 mg

Potassium 215mg

Calcium 2.8mg

Iron 2. 6mg

Vitamins (vitamin A; B-6; B-12; C; D; Riboflavin; Niacin; Thiamin; K)

Calories 38

37. Eggplant pate

Ingredients:

1 large eggplant

6 egg whites

1 tsp of mustard

1 tsp of non-fat mayonnaise

2 cloves of garlic

1 tsp of parsley

¼ cup of water

1 tsp of olive oil

Preparation:

Note: The amount of eggplant and water can vary greatly depending on the type of eggplant and ways of preparing this pate. Eggplant baked in the oven will be dry, but it will be tastier and less bitter. Eggplant cleaned and "cooked" in a microwave will be lighter, with more fluid and a little more bitter, but ready in no time.

Peel the eggplant, cut into cubes and cook together in a covered, fireproof dish in the microwave for about 5 minutes. Or, bake in a conventional oven, peel the bark, well drain of water. Add water and blend eggplant with stick-blender.

Mix mayonnaise with egg whites and olive oil. Add eggplant and blend it together.

Add finely chopped garlic and mustard. This way you can get approximately one big jar of pate. It is excellent as a spread or as a side dish. Perfect with chicken and turkey.

Nutritional values per 100g:

Carbohydrates 12.9g

Sugar 6g

Protein 17g

Total fat 3.4g

Sodium 154mg

Potassium 132.5mg

Calcium 10.4mg

Iron 3.37mg

Vitamins (vitamin A; B-6; B-12; C; D; D2; D3; K; Riboflavin; Niacin; Thiamin; K)

Calories 71

38. Stewed beef and cabbage

Ingredients:

1 large beefsteak

1 cup of chopped cabbage, cooked

¼ tsp of pepper

2 tbsp of olive oil

½ cup of water

Preparation:

Cut meat into small pieces. Put in a pot and cook on a low temperature, in olive oil until tender. Add some water if necessary. When the meat tender, add cabbage and pepper. Stew on low temperature for at least 40 minutes.

Nutritional values per 100g:

Carbohydrates 8.1g

Sugar 3.2g

Protein 36.1 g

Total fat 6.9g

Sodium 157 mg

Potassium 499mg

Calcium 19.9mg

Iron 5.9mg

Vitamins (vitamin A; B-6; B-12; C; D; D2; D3; K;Thiamin; K)

Calories 234

39. Broccoli soup

Ingredients:

1 cup of broccoli

1 small carrot

1 small onion

little salt

pepper to taste

1 tbsp of coconut oil

Preparation:

Wash the onions and carrots, but do not chop them. Put them together with the broccoli in salted water and cook. When the vegetables are done, put them all together in a blender. Remaining vegetable water heat to boiling point and stir with a little oil. Cook until the mixture thickens, add the vegetables and cook for another 5-7 minutes. Serve warm.

Nutritional values for 1 cup:

Carbohydrates 15g

Sugar 5.2g

Protein 7.2 g

Total fat 4.1g

Sodium 887 mg

Potassium 376mg

Calcium 25.5mg

Iron 1.2mg

Vitamins (vitamin A;C)

Calories 120

40. Lettuce and tuna salad

Ingredients:

1 bunch of lettuce

3 cans of tuna without oil

1 tbsp of lemon juice

2 large onions

2 large tomatoes

5 olives

Preparation:

Wash and cut lettuce. Mix it with tuna. Peel and cut the onion, cut the tomato, mix with tuna and lettuce. Add lemon juice and olives.

Nutritional values for 1 cup:

Carbohydrates 19.4g

Sugar 12g

Protein 31.2g

Total fat (good monounsaturated fat) 11.5g

Sodium 141mg

Potassium 86.1mg

Calcium 43.2mg

Iron 0.31mg

Vitamins (vitamin A; B-6; B-12; C; D; D2; D3; K; Riboflavin; Niacin; Thiamin; K)

Calories 71

41. Grilled trout fillets with parsley

Ingredients:

3 thick trout fillets

1 tbsp of parsley

3 tbsp of olive oil

6 cloves of garlic

Preparation:

Mix chopped garlic with parsley and olive oil. Spread it over fish and fry in a barbecue pan for about 15-20 minutes, on both sides. Remove from the pan and use a kitchen paper to soak the excess oil.

Nutritional values per 100g:

Carbohydrates 0.2g

Sugar 0

Protein 25.2 g

Total fat 6.6g

Sodium 113.8 mg

Potassium 61mg

Calcium 29mg

Iron 0.33mg

Vitamins (vitamin A; B-6; B-12; C; D; D2; D3; K; Riboflavin; Niacin; Thiamin; K)

Calories 170

42. Cauliflower soup

Ingredients:

1 cup of cauliflower

1 small carrot

1 small onion

little pepper

1 tbsp of oil

Preparation:

Wash the onions and carrots, but do not chop them. Put them together with the cauliflower in water and cook. When the vegetables are done, put them all together in a blender. Remaining vegetable water heat to boiling point and stir with a little oil. Cook until the mixture thickens, add the vegetables and cook for another 5-7 minutes. Serve warm.

Nutritional values for 1 cup:

Carbohydrates 13g

Sugar 4.2g

Protein 6.2 g

Total fat 4.4g

Sodium 862 mg

Potassium 366mg

Calcium 24.1mg

Iron 2mg

Vitamins (vitamin A;C)

Calories 118

43. Tomato omelet

Ingredients:

3 eggs

1 large tomato

1 small onion

1 tsp of olive oil

salt to taste

Preparation:

Wash and cut tomato. Peel and cut the onion. Fry tomato and onion in olive oil for about 10-15 minutes, on a low temperature. Remove from the heat when the water evaporates. Add eggs and mix well. Fry for another 2 minutes.

Nutritional values per 100 g:

Carbohydrates 6.1g

Sugar 2g

Protein 20g

Total fat (good monounsaturated fat) 12g

Sodium 176mg

Potassium 173mg

Calcium 15.9mg

Iron 1.9mg

Vitamins (vitamin A; B-6; B-12; C)

Calories 184

44. Grilled salmon fillet

Ingredients:

1 large salmon fillet

1 tbsp of lemon juice

2 tbsp of olive oil

1 tbsp of ground chili pepper

Preparation:

Wash the fillet and pat dry using a kitchen paper. Sprinkle some lemon juice on it and fry in a small barbecue pan for about 15-20 minutes, on a very high temperature. Remove from the pan and soak the excess oil with a kitchen paper. Add ground chili pepper before serving.

Nutritional values per 100 g:

Carbohydrates 2.9

Sugar 0.8g

Protein 24g

Total fat (good monounsaturated fat) 14.6g

Sodium 63mg

Potassium 374mg

Calcium 0.9mg

Iron 1.8mg

Vitamins (vitamin A; B-6; B-12; C)

Calories 220

45. Mixed vegetable salad:

Ingredients:

1 bunch of lettuce

1 small carrot

1 medium tomato

1 medium onion

1 small cucumber

1 medium eggplant

1 medium zucchini

1 tbsp of olive oil

1 tsp of lemon juice

Preparation:

Peel and cut eggplant and zucchini. Fry it in olive oil for 8-10 minutes. Remove from pan and soak excess oil with kitchen paper. Meanwhile, wash and cut vegetables into small pieces. Mix eggplant and zucchini with other vegetables and season with olive oil and lemon juice.

Nutritional values for one cup:

Carbohydrates 12.3g

Sugar 8.9g

Protein 11.2 g

Total fat (good monounsaturated fat) 6.5g

Sodium 176.3 mg

Potassium 95mg

Calcium 63.5mg

Iron 0.74mg

Vitamins (vitamin A; B-6; B-12; C; D; D2; D3; K; Riboflavin; Niacin; Thiamin; K)

Calories 51

46. Grilled calamari in curry sauce

Ingredients:

1 cup of frozen calamari rings

¼ cup of water

1 tsp of curry

2 tbsp of olive oil

2 cloves of garlic

1 tsp of chopped parsley

Preparation:

Make a sauce with chopped water, garlic, parsley, curry and olive oil. Fry calamari rings in a barbecue pan without oil for 7-10 minutes, on a medium temperature. You want to get a nice golden color. Add the sauce to barbecue pan with calamari and fry for few more minutes. You can add some more water if your sauce is too thick.

Nutritional values per 100g:

Carbohydrates 0.2g

Sugar 0g

Protein 19.8 g

Total fat (good monounsaturated fat) 2.8g

Sodium 96.3 mg

Potassium 0.3mg

Calcium 1.5mg

Iron 0.7mg

Vitamins (vitamin A; BD; D2; K)

Calories 92

47. Grilled sardines

Ingredients:

1 small pack (200g) of frozen sardines

4 cloves of garlic

4 tbsp of olive oil

3 tsp of tumeric

½ tsp of salt

Preparation:

Defrost and wash sardines. Make a garlic sauce with garlic, olive oil and tumeric. Spread it over sardines and fry in a barbecue pan without extra oil for about 20 minutes on a medium temperature. They should have golden-brow color before serving. Salt to taste.

Nutritional values per 100g:

Carbohydrates 0.2g

Sugar 0g

Protein 19 g

Total fat (good monounsaturated fat) 6g

Sodium 225.3 mg

Potassium 3mg

Calcium 3.5mg

Iron 3.2mg

Vitamins (vitamin A; B-6; D; D2; D3; K; Riboflavin; Niacin; Thiamin; K)

Calories 130

48. Banana shake

Ingredients:

1 large banana

2 egg whites

1.5 cup of water

1 tsp of vanilla extract

1 tbsp of agave syrup

Preparation:

Peel and chop banana into small cubes. Combine with other ingredients in a blender and mix for 30 seconds, until smooth mixture. Keep in the refrigerator and serve cold.

Nutritional values for 1 glass:

Carbohydrates 8g

Sugar 4.9g

Protein 10.2g

Total fat 2.67g

Sodium 74mg

Potassium 512.9mg

Calcium 79mg

Iron 1.88mg

Vitamins (Vitamin B-6; B-12; D; D-D2+D3)

Calories 56

49. Grilled green peppers

Ingredients:

2 green peppers

1 tbsp of olive oil

2 cloves of garlic

chopped parsley

Preparation:

Mix the olive oil with garlic and parsley. Spread the sauce over peppers and fry in a barbecue pan on a low temperature for about 10-15 minutes. Stir constantly.

Nutritional values per 100g:

Carbohydrates 5g

Sugar 2.2g

Protein 1.8 g

Total fat 0.4g

Sodium 4.3 mg

Potassium 191mg

Calcium 2.5mg

Iron 1.8mg

Vitamins (vitamin A; B-6; B-12; C; D; D2; D3; K; Riboflavin; Niacin; Thiamin; K)

Calories 27

50. Seafood salad

Ingredients:

1 small pack (200g) of frozen mixed seafood

3 tbsp of olive oil

1 medium onion

¼ tsp of salt

¼ cup of water (optional)

Preparation

Fry frozen seafood without oil until tender (try the octopus, it takes the most time to tender). You can add some water if necessary. Remove from frying pan and allow it to cool for about an hour. Peel and finely chop the onion. Mix it with seafood and add olive oil. This salad is best cold. Let it stand in the refrigerator for few hours before serving.

Nutritional values per 1 cup:

Carbohydrates 3.45g

Sugar 1.68g

Protein 25.8 g

Total fat 16.4g

Sodium 827mg

Potassium 453mg

Calcium 13.5mg

Iron 10mg

Vitamins (Vitamin C; B-6; B-12; A-RAE; A-IU; E; D; D-D2+D3; K; Thianin; Riboflavin; Niacin)

Calories 280

51. Grilled zucchini with garlic

Ingredients:

1 large zucchini

4 cloves of garlic

1 tbsp of olive oil

¼ tsp of salt

Preparation:

Peel and cut zucchini into thick slices. Chop garlic and fry it for few minutes in olive oil, until nice gold color. Add zucchini and fry for another 10 minutes on a low temperature. Sprinkle with some chopped parsley before serving. Salt to taste.

Nutritional values for 1 slice:

Carbohydrates 3.6g

Sugar 1.9g

Protein 2.9 g

Total fat 0.9g

Sodium 2.21 mg

Potassium 354mg

Calcium 0.12mg

Iron 0.2mg

Vitamins (vitamin A; B-6; B-12; C; D:K)

Calories 25

52. Baked apples

Ingredients:

2 large apples

1 tsp of cinnamon

Preparation:

Bake the apples at 300 degrees for 15 minutes. Sprinkle with cinnamon before serving.

Nutritional values per 100g:

Carbohydrates 14.8g

Sugar 10g

Protein 0.4 g

Total fat 0.3g

Sodium 1.7mg

Potassium 108mg

Calcium 0mg

Iron 0mg

Vitamins (vitamin A; C)

Calories 53

53. Grilled steak with pineapple slices

Ingredients:

1 large steak

7 pineapple slices

1 tsp of ginger

little water

pepper to taste

Preparation:

Fry pineapple slices for 5-10 minutes, slightly adding a little water. Remove pineapple slices from a frying pan and fry the steak in the same frying pan for 15-20 minutes. You can add some water while frying steak. Serve with pineapple slices and sprinkle with ginger. Pepper to taste

Nutritional values per 100g:

Carbohydrates 3.8g

Sugar 2.1g

Protein 32.9 g

Total fat 4.9g

Sodium 64 mg

Potassium 413mg

Calcium 0mg

Iron 17.8mg

Vitamins (vitamin A; B-6; B-12; C; D)

Calories 182

54. Cooked cauliflower in mint sauce

Ingredients:

1 medium cauliflower

1 tbsp of chopped mint leaves

1 tsp of ginger

1 tbsp of agave syrup

Preparation:

Clean and cut cauliflower into medium cubes. Cook it in water until tender. Remove from pot and drain well. Meanwhile, make a sauce with agave syrup, ginger and mint, by combining all the ingredients in a small bowl. Pour it over cauliflower and allow it to cool for a while before serving.

Nutritional values per 100g:

Carbohydrates 6.8g

Sugar 2.8g

Protein 1.9 g

Total fat 0.4g

Sodium 31 mg

Potassium 301mg

Calcium 2.7mg

Iron 2.3mg

Vitamins (vitamin C; K)

Calories 29

55. Mushroom soup

Ingredients:

1 cup of fresh button mushrooms

1 small carrot

1 small onion

¼ tsp of pepper

1 tbsp of oil

Preparation:

Wash the onions and carrots, but do not chop them. Put them together in a large pot, add water to cover the vegetables and cook until tender. When the vegetables are done, mix them with mushrooms and put all together in a blender. Remaining vegetable water heat to boiling point and stir with a little oil. Cook until the mixture thickens, add the vegetables and cook for another 5-7 minutes. You can decorate it with little parsley.

Nutritional values for 1 cup:

Carbohydrates 3.3g

Sugar 0.2g

Protein 1.9 g

Total fat 2.6g

Sodium 340 mg

Potassium 31mg

Calcium 0mg

Iron 0mg

Vitamins (vitamin D;K)

Calories 41

56. Trout fillet with almond and tumeric sauce

Ingredients:

1 thin slice of trout fillet

1 tsp of tumeric

1 tbsp of olive oil

½ cup of almonds

1 tsp of dried rosemary

¼ tsp of pepper

Preparation:

Wash and dry the fillet. Sprinkle with tumeric and fry in hot oil for few minutes on each side. Remove from frying pan. Make a sauce with almonds, olive oil, rosemary and pepper. Pour the sauce over the fillet and fry for another few minutes, until golden brown color.

Nutritional values per 100g:

Carbohydrates 3.7g

Sugar 0.2g

Protein 25g

Total fat 8.6g

Sodium 62 mg

Potassium 263mg

Calcium 10mg

Iron 2.5mg

Vitamins (vitamin A; B-6; B-12; C; D:K)

Calories 173

57. Trout soup

Ingredients:

1 large trout

2 small carrots

1 tbsp of olive oil

1 tsp of dried parsley

dill to taste

Preparation:

Wash and clean the fish (remove all bones). Cook the fish in a large pot for about 20. After the fish is done, add a little olive oil (just to cover the bottom). Fry chopped carrots for few minutes and add water, parsley and dill. Cook for another 15 minutes. After about 15 minutes add the fish (whole or cut into large chunks). Put in each plate 1 tsp of olive oil and pour the soup.

Nutritional values per 1 cup:

Carbohydrates 3.4g

Sugar 0.9g

Protein 5.9 g

Total fat 2g

Sodium 365 mg

Potassium 123mg

Calcium 2.3mg

Iron 2.3mg

Vitamins (vitamin A; B-6; B-12; C)

Calories 46

58. Cucumber salad

Ingredients:

3 large cucumbers

6 tbsp of grated walnuts

3 tbsp of sesame seeds oil

Preparation:

Peel and cut the cucumbers into thin slices. Season with sesame seed oil and sprinkle with grated walnuts.

Nutritional values per 100g:

Carbohydrates 6.8g

Sugar 2.7g

Protein 5.9 g

Total fat 4.9g

Sodium 5.76 mg

Potassium 213mg

Calcium 5.27mg

Iron 2.1mg

Vitamins (vitamin A; B-6; B-12; C; D:K)

Calories 34

59. Grilled mushrooms with garlic sauce

Ingredients:

3 cups of fresh button mushrooms

6 cloves of garlic

3 tbsp of olive oil

¼ tsp of pepper

Preparation:

Fry mushrooms without oil in a barbecue pan on a low temperature until all the water evaporates. Meanwhile, chop garlic, add to frying pan and mix with mushrooms. Fry for few more minutes. Sprinkle with olive oil before serving. Add some pepper to taste. Serve warm.

Nutritional values for one cup:

Carbohydrates 5.2g

Sugar 1.3g

Protein 8.2 g

Total fat (good monounsaturated fat) 2.3g

Sodium 47.3 mg

Potassium 25.1mg

Calcium 13.1mg

Iron 0.61mg

Vitamins (vitamin A; B-6; B-12; C; D; D2; D3; K; Riboflavin; Niacin; Thiamin; K)

Calories 98

60. Apple and carrot balls with cinnamon

Ingredients:

5 large apples

3 large carrots

6 tsp of cinnamon

6 tsp of agave syrup

3 tsp of lemon juice

Preparation:

Peel and grate apples and carrots. Combine with other ingredients in a blender to get a smooth mixture. Make little balls and allow them to cool them in the refrigerator for few hours.

You can add grated walnuts or almonds to this recipe. That is optional, but it will increase the proteins.

Nutritional values per 100g:

Carbohydrates 17.2g

Sugar 15.3g

Protein 9.1 g

Total fat (good monounsaturated fat) 2.3g

Sodium 147.4 mg

Potassium 625mg

Calcium 13.1mg

Iron 11.61mg

Vitamins (vitamin A; B-6; B-12; C; D; D2; D3; K; Riboflavin; Niacin; Thiamin; K)

Calories 78

61. Grilled eggplant with parsley

Ingredients:

1 small eggplant

½ cup of chopped parsley

1 tsp of olive oil

Preparation:

Peel the eggplant and cut into slices. Bake it in a barbecue pan without oil. When done, spread olive oil over it, sprinkle with parsley.

Nutritional values per slice:

Carbohydrates 7.9g

Sugar .4

Protein 7.2g

Total fat 2.21g

Sodium 53mg

Potassium 29.1mg

Calcium 13.1mg

Iron 0.38mg

Vitamins (vitamin A; B-6; B-12; C; D; D2; D3; K; Riboflavin; Niacin; Thiamin; K)

Calories 52

62. Steak salad with mushrooms

Ingredients:

1 large steak

3 cups of button mushrooms

6 tbsp of chopped parsley

1 bunch of lettuce

1 large tomato

1 large onion

1 large cucumber

4 tbsp of olive oil

Preparation:

Fry the steak without oil for 15-20 minutes. Remove from pan and cut it into medium sized pieces. Fry the mushrooms, but don't cut them. Wash and peel vegetables, mix with steak and mushrooms. Season with little olive or sesame oil.

Nutritional values for one cup:

Carbohydrates 18.6g

Sugar 11.3g

Protein 21.9g

Total fat (good monounsaturated fat) 14.2g

Sodium 153.3 mg

Potassium 89.8mg

Calcium 49.9mg

Iron 0.42mg

Vitamins (vitamin A; B-6; B-12; C; D; D2; D3; K; Riboflavin; Niacin; Thiamin; K)

Calories 79

63. Fruit shake

Ingredients:

1 cup of strawberries

1 large banana

1 slice of watermelon

½ tsp of cinnamon

½ cup of water

¼ cup of ground walnuts

Preparation:

Mix ingredients in a blender for about 30 seconds. Sprinkle with cinnamon and allow it to cool in the refrigerator for about 30 minutes. Serve with ice.

Nutritional values for 1 glass:

Carbohydrates 10.67g

Sugar 8.11g

Protein 8.65g

Total fat 2.54g

Sodium 95mg

Potassium 159.6mg

Calcium 93mg

Iron 1.03mg

Vitamins (Vitamin C total ascorbic acid; B-6; B-12; A-RAE; A-IU; E-alpha-tocopherol; D; K-phylloquinone; Thianin; Riboflavin; Niacin)

Calories 74.6

64. Veal cutlet with almonds

Ingredients:

1 veal cutlet

½ cup of grated almonds

¼ tsp of pepper

1 tsp of sesame oil

½ cup of water

Preparation:

Mix almonds, pepper and water. Cook it for about 10 minutes. Remove from heat and cool it. Wash and dry cutlet. Fry it in oil for about 15-20 minutes. Add almond sauce before serving.

Nutritional values per 100g:

Carbohydrates 4.6g

Sugar 4.2g

Protein 29.6 g

Total fat 11.4g

Sodium 133 mg

Potassium 234mg

Calcium 2.3mg

Iron 2.13mg

Vitamins (vitamin A; B-6; B-12; C; D; D2; D3; K; Riboflavin; Niacin; Thiamin; K)

Calories 217

65. Spinach omelet

Ingredients:

1 cup of chopped spinach

2 eggs

olive oil for frying

Preparation:

Cook spinach in salted water until tender. Remove from pan and drain. Fry in olive oil for 5-6 minutes and add eggs. Mix well and serve warm.

Nutritional values per 100g:

Carbohydrates 0.98g

Sugar 0.44g

Protein 12.1g

Total fat 14.4g

Sodium 256mg

Potassium 217.4mg

Calcium 5.6mg

Iron 11.37mg

Vitamins (vitamin A; B-6; D; D2; D3)

Calories 143

66. Squids stuffed with walnuts

Ingredients:

2 large squids

½ cup of grated walnuts

1 tsp of lemon juice

½ tsp of ginger

1 tbsp of olive oil

Preparation:

Wash and clean the squids. Mix walnuts, lemon juice and ginger and stuff squids. Place in greased pan and cover with baking foil. Bake for 20 minutes in preheated oven, at 200 degrees. Remove the foil and bake for another 5-10 minutes.

Nutritional values per 100g:

Carbohydrates 0.2g

Sugar 0g

Protein 19.8 g

Total fat (good monounsaturated fat) 2.8g

Sodium 96.3 mg

Potassium 0.3mg

Calcium 1.5mg

Iron 0.7mg

Vitamins (vitamin A; BD; D2; K)

Calories 92

67. Tomato and garlic soup

Ingredients:

1 cup of tomato sauce

2 cups of water

2 cloves of garlic

2 tbsp of olive oil

1 tsp of dried marjoram

Preparation:

Fry finely chopped garlic in oil for about 10 minutes. Stir in tomato sauce mixed with water. Let it boil for 7-10 minutes. Serve with marjoram.

Nutritional values per 150ml:

Carbohydrates 7.9g

Sugar 4.1g

Protein 7.9g

Total fat 0.9g

Sodium 195.3 mg

Potassium 117mg

Calcium 0.3mg

Iron 2.8mg

Vitamins (vitamin A; C)

Calories 39

68. Lamb cutlet with basil

Ingredients:

1 thick lamb cutlet

1 tsp of chopped basil

pepper to taste

1 tbsp of sesame oil

Preparation:

Fry cutlet in sesame oil for 15 minutes. Remove from pan and soak up excess oil. Sprinkle with pepper and basil.

Nutritional values per 100g:

Carbohydrates 5.9g

Sugar 4.5g

Protein 29.3 g

Total fat 11.9g

Sodium 129 mg

Potassium 241mg

Calcium 2.93mg

Iron 2.17mg

Vitamins (vitamin A; B-6; B-12; C; D; D2; D3; K; Riboflavin; Niacin; Thiamin; K)

Calories 210

69. Grilled mushrooms in tomato sauce

Ingredients:

1 cup of button mushrooms

1 large tomato

1 tsp of olive oil

2 cloves of garlic

1 tbsp of fresh basil

Preparation:

Wash and cut tomato. Chop garlic and mix with tomato and fresh basil. Cook it in olive oil and little water for about 10-15 minutes, on low temperature. Grill mushrooms without oil in a barbecue pan for 5 minutes. Add to tomato sauce and mix well.

Nutritional values for one cup:

Carbohydrates 5.1g

Sugar 2.7g

Protein 6.1 g

Total fat 1.8g

Sodium 46.1 mg

Potassium 24.1mg

Calcium 13.5mg

Iron 0.62mg

Vitamins (vitamin A; B-6; B-12; C; D; D2; D3; K; Riboflavin; Niacin; Thiamin; K)

Calories 108

70. Shrimp skewers

Ingredients:

6 frozen shrimps

6 cherry tomatoes

6 eggplant cubes

6 green pepper cubes

olive oil

½ tsp of oregano

2 wooden sticks

Preparation:

Put the ingredients on 2 wooden sticks – 1 shrimp, 1 tomato, 1 eggplant cube, 1 green pepper cube. Repeat the process until you use all the ingredients. Sprinkle with olive oil and oregano and fry in a barbecue pan for 5-10 minutes.

Nutritional values per 100g:

Carbohydrates 7.1g

Sugar 4.3g

Protein 29g

Total fat (good monounsaturated fat) 1.42g

Sodium 132mg

Potassium 279.1mg

Calcium 8.4mg

Iron 4.32mg

Vitamins (vitamin A; B-6; B-12; C; D; D2; D3; K; Riboflavin; Niacin; Thiamin; K)

Calories 154

Other Great Titles by This Author

www.ingramcontent.com/pod-product-compliance
Lightning Source LLC
Chambersburg PA
CBHW071735080526
44588CB00013B/2039